DIARY

OF A
MINECRAFT
ENDER DRAGON

BOOKS KID

TABLE OF CONTENTS

Day 1

It was a day that started just like any other. Wake up. Burp. Laugh at the little flame that comes out. Scratch my back before I stretch, stand up, walk around my nest a bit while I consider getting up before flopping back down again for a bit more sleep.

It's a tough life being an Ender dragon.

When I eventually dragged myself out of bed, I went for my usual flap around The End. There's not an awful lot to see out here. Just a floating island with a bunch of Endermen wandering around on it.

"Morning, Jo!" I called down to one of them.

"Morning, Ember!" he yelled back as I flew overhead. "It's a good day to be in The End."

"Isn't it?" I replied.

We have exactly the same chat every day. Endermen aren't exactly known for their brilliant conversation skills. I suppose it's because nothing ever happens here. Oh sure, we get the odd Minecraftian coming down, thinking they can defeat me and steal my eggs, but they never do. I could build a nest out of the remains of Minecraftians who'd thought they could beat me. I'm just that tough.

I heard a small "whomp!" It was the sound of a Minecraftian arriving through one of their portals. I sighed and prepared myself for battle. I suppose a fight would make today a little more interesting, but I knew exactly how it was going to go. The Minecraftian would hide behind an obsidian column while they prepared their bow and arrows. They'd fire a few shots, thinking it would wear me down and then dash about, trying to avoid my attacks while they get in a few blows with their swords.

It's impossible for a Minecraftian to defeat me by themselves. I usually let them get a few hits in, just to lull them into a false sense of security and make them feel good about themselves before I swoop in and finish them off.

Contrary to popular belief, Minecraftians really don't taste very nice, not even with tomato sauce and chips.

I waited all day, but the Minecraftian didn't attack me. It was very odd, not to mention annoying. I'm going to have to stay awake all night to make sure they don't try to get me in my sleep.

Day 2

The Minecraftian didn't attack me during the night. Good thing too, because I fell asleep after a while, so I could have woken up to a Minecraftian axe in my face.

I did my usual burp, laugh, and stretch routine before heading out to see if I could find him in the End. Maybe he'd left once he'd realized how boring it is here.

This is one weird Minecraftian. He's built a camp and he looks like he's going to be staying here for a while. Why would he do that? Much as I love living in The End because of the peace and quiet, it really isn't the most exciting of places for a Minecraftian. Don't they like building things? I thought that's what all Minecraftians did. There's not much you can use to build with here. And if he wanted to start a fight, well, we already know that he doesn't stand a chance against me and there are too many Endermen for him to be able to take them all on by himself. Hurt one of them and you'll get the whole team fighting back. Nobody in their right mind would attack an Enderman.

I shall have to watch this one. Maybe he's got some sort of weird machine or a new type of potion or something that will help him fight me. I think I'll go right up to him and see if I can see any strange weapons on him. First, though, I'm going to move my eggs away somewhere safe, somewhere you can only get to by flying. That way, even if he does try to fight me, he won't be able to steal my precious eggs.

I don't like having a Minecraftian loose in The End. It's a bit like someone walking into your house, putting their feet up on the sofa and helping themselves to all your biscuits. He doesn't belong here and if he's not gone by tomorrow, then I might just have to do something about him.

Day 3

He hasn't left yet. In fact, he's been cooking food and whistling!

That's it. I decided I was going to deal with this Minecraftian once and for all.

I flew down to his camp, deliberately flapping my wings so that his fire went out.

Calmly, the Minecraftian started his fire again. "I'm just cooking up some food," he said. "Do you want some?"

Food? Offering me food?

"I am the mighty Ender Dragon!" I cried. "Hear me roar!"

"No thanks," replied the Minecraftian. "I'm sure you can be very noisy and I don't like loud noises. Let's just say you did and leave it at that."

"What?"

"I know, I know, you're the great big Ender Dragon, you're very scary, you're very difficult to fight, blah, blah, blah. Everyone knows all that. But I want to know the *real* Ender Dragon. I'm sure you're a very nice person behind all the roaring and fighting, and I'd love to get to know you. Want some rabbit?"

He held out some meat and I was so stunned, I took it without thinking.

"My name's Dirk," said the Minecraftian. "What's yours?"

"Ember," I replied, taking a bite out of the rabbit. It melted in my mouth. I'd never tasted anything like it. "Oh my goodness. This is delicious!"

"I thought you might enjoy it," smiled Dirk. "I figured you didn't get much variety down here, so you would appreciate some different food."

"It's out of this world," I told him. "Have you got any more?"

"Sure."

Dirk reached into his bag and tossed me some more rabbit meat. "I've got some pork chops as well if you'd like."

Would I?

By the time I'd finished eating, I'd had five rabbits, three pork chops, a piece of pumpkin pie (I didn't like that much), and a melon. "That was amazing." I lay back, patting my full belly, burping a little fiery burp. "You can come here again if you bring more food like that."

"I was hoping you'd feel that way." Dirk reached into his bag to get something and I was instantly on high alert. Had he just been trying to get me to relax so that he could attack me?

He pulled out a notepad and pen. "You see, I'm a writer," he explained, "and I want to write a book about you."

A book? About me?

"Why would you want to do that?" I asked. "Aren't there already lots of books about Ender Dragons?"

"Sure," nodded Dirk. "*How to kill an Ender Dragon in three easy steps*, *Strategies for defeating the Ender Dragon*, *Top tips for how to fight the Ender Dragon and win*, *The idiot's guide to destroying the Ender Dragon...*" He shrugged. "Do I need to go on?"

I shook my head. I couldn't believe it. People actually wrote books about how to fight me? Since nobody had ever defeated me, the people writing them obviously didn't have a clue about how to beat me, yet Minecraftians must be buying them or nobody would write them.

"So you've come to try out some new fighting methods, have you?" I growled.

"Oh, no, no, no!" Dirk shook his head, dropping his pen and paper to hold up his hands in surrender. "I don't want to fight you."

"Really? Since every other Minecraftian who's ever come here has attacked me, what makes you so different?"

"I told you. I want to write a book about what it's like to be an Ender Dragon."

"I'm already doing that," I informed him loftily. "It's called my diary. Whatever you come up with won't be better than that."

Dirk picked up his notepad, tapping his pen against it thoughtfully. "Well, if you're already writing a diary, why don't we do something that's worth writing about in it? I don't mean to be rude, but I'm guessing that all you ever put in your diary is that you spent the day flying around The End and fighting the odd Minecraftian who comes down here. Am I right?"

I blushed, but I had to admit that he had a point. I had quite a few books filled with 'Woke up. Flew around. Went to bed.' In fact, now that I thought about it, I wondered why I bothered keeping a diary when there wasn't really anything important I needed to remember.

"So why don't we go away for a bit?" Dirk suggested. "I could show you the sights of Minecraftia. You'll be able to explore the world and at the end of it, you'll have a diary you'll enjoy looking back on for years to come, and I'll be able to write a book about Ender Dragons that will be completely different from anything out there. People will come flocking to The End, but not because they want to kill you. They'll all want to be your best friend because you're so cool. Does that sound like a good idea?"

I nodded slowly. "I have always wanted to see what it was like in the Overworld." Dirk looked at me pleadingly and I made up my mind. "All right. I'll come with you. But if there's any sign that you're trying to trick me and you're really just after my eggs, then I'll swallow you whole. You'll taste great with some chips and tomato sauce."

Dirk turned pale and I was sure I saw his knees knocking together. I grinned to myself. Dirk didn't need to know that I hated the taste of Minecraftians.

Day 4

"Do you have everything you need for the journey?" asked Dirk, as he started building a strange device. It looked a little like a door that went nowhere.

I looked around. I wasn't sure what I was supposed to be taking with me. I don't need any weapons, Dirk had promised me plenty of Minecraftian food, and I could make a nest from resources in Minecraftia. My eggs were safe where I'd hidden them and I wasn't going to risk taking them anywhere. "I guess so."

"OK, well, fingers crossed that this works."

"What do you mean, fingers crossed?"

Dirk looked embarrassed. "Well, all the books say that if you want to get out of The End, you have to kill the Ender Dragon."

I growled at him.

"But I don't think that's true," Dirk added hurriedly. "I'm sure there must be a way to leave The End *with* the Ender Dragon, so I've done lots of reading and practicing making portals, and I'm pretty certain that this is going to work."

"Pretty certain?"

"Well, there's always the chance that nothing will happen."

"I suppose if that's the worst that could happen, that's not so bad."

Dirk shuffled his feet about a bit. "That's not exactly the worst thing that could happen."

"It isn't? What is, then?"

"We could both instantly disintegrate the moment we step into the portal."

Disintegrate? I didn't like the sound of that.

"But I'm sure that won't happen," Dirk added hurriedly. "Well, pretty sure, anyway..."

"Pretty sure, pretty certain." I shook my head. "If we disintegrate, it won't be pretty at all!"

Dirk lit a fire in the center of the portal and stepped back as it started to burn a peculiar purple color. "There we go!" he smiled. "It's all working just the way I hoped it would." He started throwing a few ingredients into the fire, muttering and mumbling as he did so. I had no idea what he was doing and I was getting bored. It was a stupid idea anyway to think that I could go on holiday with a Minecraftian.

Just as I was about to fly off, Dirk let out a loud cheer. "Woo-hoo! It worked!"

The door frame now contained a portal that glowed with an eerie indigo hue. "Come on," said Dirk, picking up his bag. "We need to go through now while the portal is open. I don't know how long it will last. After you."

"No, after you." If there was going to be any disintegrating round here, I wanted Dirk to be the one who vanished.

"All right then." Dirk took a deep breath and stepped forward into the portal.

"Dirk? Are you all right, Dirk? You haven't disintegrated, have you?"

There was no reply.

I walked all around the portal, but there was no sign of him. Either he'd disintegrated or his portal had worked and he was in Minecraftia. But how was I to know what had happened to him?

I hadn't really thought things through when I told him to go first.

There was only one way to find out what had happened to Dirk. I took a deep breath, flapped my wings a few times and went forward into the portal.

Day 5

Going through portals is weird. Minecraftia is weird. Everything about my life right now is weird.

As you can probably tell, I did not disintegrate when I went through the portal. I popped out on the other side where there was an identical frame resting on some rock. Dirk was standing there, waiting for me, a big grin on his face.

"I told you it would be all right!" he said.

"Yes, well, it made my tummy do little flip flops," I replied grumpily. "I don't want to do that again any time soon."

"You won't have to," Dirk assured me. "We have a whole world to explore first."

I looked around. It was like nothing I'd ever seen before. The ground was green and the sky was blue with a big round light in the middle of it.

"What a strange torch," I commented.

Dirk looked up and laughed. "That's not a torch. It's the sun!"

"The sun," I repeated. I'd heard of it but I hadn't believed it really existed until now. No sunlight reached The End. "And what are those?"

I nodded towards some brown things growing out of the ground with green on top.

"Those? They're trees."

I moved over to take a closer look, but as I reached forward to sniff at the bark, I accidentally touched the tree and it disappeared!

"Uh-oh," said Dirk. "I'd heard that this might be a possibility, but I was hoping it wasn't true."

"Hoping what wasn't true?"

"There are legends that tell of a time when Ender Dragons left The End and roamed free throughout Minecraftia. So powerful were the dragons that anything they touched, they destroyed without even thinking about it."

Well, I hadn't been thinking about destroying the tree, so that much was true.

"This might be a problem." Dirk thought, tapping his foot. "A-ha! I think I have an idea. Stay on the rock and don't touch anything. I'll be back as soon as I can."

With that, he ran off into the trees, leaving me standing there, trying not to touch anything else.

Day 6

"I look ridiculous." I still couldn't believe that I'd let Dirk talk me into putting on the stupid outfit he'd made for me.

"I think it's rather fetching," he assured me. "Especially given the limited materials I had to work with."

He'd made me an outfit out of stone, and to say that it was heavy and difficult to move in didn't even go half way to describing just how uncomfortable it was.

"Anyway, you don't really have much of a choice," he went on. "If you don't cover yourself up, you're going to destroy all of Minecraftia. You'll get used to it soon enough."

I tried moving, the rocks bashing and crashing into each other. "I've never heard of armor meant to protect everyone except the person wearing it," I complained. 'This is dumb.'

"Well if someone attacks you, you have my permission to take it off right away," Dirk told me.

"Gee, thanks."

Day 7

I had to admit that Dirk's idea worked, although it's a good thing that Ender Dragons are so strong. Anyone else carrying around this much weight in stones and bedrock would struggle to keep going for long.

Once I got used to not being quite as agile as normal, it wasn't so bad and I even managed to start flying again.

Wow. The views across Minecraftia from the sky are amazing. Up in the air, I could see for miles and miles. I could see where the forest ended and the plains began, with mountains in the distance with a dusting of white across the top of them. Yellow flowers dotted about the plains, bringing a certain cheer to the place. I'd never seen anything so beautiful.

It couldn't be more different than The End. There are colors everywhere and the smells, the delicious smells!

I closed my eyes and breathed deeply, wanting to drink it all in. Everything was so fresh and so new. I didn't think I'd ever get tired of being here.

Day 8

"I'm tired of being here," I moaned at Dirk. "The armor is really heavy and it's making my wings hurt. I can only fly for five minutes at a time and walking takes forever. How you Minecraftians put up with having to walk everywhere, I don't know."

Dirk laughed. "It's not that bad. But then again, I've never flown anywhere so I don't know what that's like."

"You've never flown?" I looked at him, eyes wide. "Then you've never lived!"

"Humans aren't meant to fly," he replied simply. "If we were, then we'd just make wings out of wood and feathers and soar over the trees."

"Or you'd climb on the back of a friendly Ender Dragon," I grinned.

"Are you serious?" I don't think I'd ever seen someone look as excited as Dirk did. He was like a little kid opening his birthday presents.

"Sure. Jump up."

It took a few moments of huffing and puffing for Dirk to figure out the best way of climbing onto my back with all the armor in the way, but at last, he was perched safely.

"Wow, Dirk. You're a lot heavier than you look," I complained. "I'm going to need a long run up to get off the ground."

Either Dirk didn't care or he was pretending not to hear me as I looked around to find a good place to get some speed up.

At last, I found the perfect spot. The ground was flat with no trees in the way while I built up enough speed to get into the air.

"Hold on tight, Dirk, because here we go!"

The ground shook as my feet pounded along while I ran faster and faster, trying to get enough momentum to fly. As I raced along, my wings flapped, sending gusts of wind through the forest. Chickens clucked, cows mooed, and all the animals tried to get as far away from me as possible so that they wouldn't get hurt by my powerful wings.

We rose off the ground a little, but went back down again. "You're too heavy!" I called up. "I'm going to have to ditch some of the armor."

Dirk yelled something back, but I couldn't hear him with the wind blowing past my ears. I reached under my chest and undid the buckles holding the armor around my legs. As it fell to the ground, I immediately felt as though I was as light as a feather, even though I still had most of my armor on. All that stone really did weigh a lot.

"Look out for that-!"

I could feel Dirk ducking as we went crashing into a bush, but now that the armor covering my legs was gone, it simply disappeared when I touched it.

At last, I could feel myself going higher and higher, my wings beating strongly as I finally managed to get off the ground.

"Woo-hoo!"

I could hear Dirk's delighted cries as he leaned from side to side to see Minecraftia like he never had before. "This is amazing!" he called to me. "You're right! Flying is much better than walking! We should fly everywhere!"

I chuckled. Of course I was right. I always am.

Day 9

We can't fly everywhere, much as I want to. For a start, it would make my holiday really, really short. Half the point of being here is for me to explore Minecraftia, and if I was flying all the time, I'd miss out on seeing all the things on the ground like the beautiful flowers and weird animals.

The other problem is getting down again. You see, I hadn't thought about that when I took my armor off so I could give Dirk a ride. It's a bit of a problem when Ender Dragons destroy almost any type of blocks they come in contact with. As I came in to land, the earth disappeared under my feet until I finally hit the bedrock.

There is a very, very deep ravine in the middle of the sunflower plains now.

"Stay here," Dirk ordered. "I'm going to go and find your armor."

"But that's going to take ages," I told him. "We flew for miles. If you walk back from here, it's going to take you days if not weeks to get back to where we left that armor."

"Darn it. You're right." Dirk thought about it. "Look, I'm just going to have to make some more. I think I saw something not far from here that will do the job. Just stay put until I get back."

I shrugged my shoulders. "Do you think you could get me something to eat while you're at it? It's been ages since I had anything to eat."

Dirk looked at me. "How can you be hungry? You ate two whole cows for breakfast."

"Yes, well, dragons have a big appetite. It's not my fault. I can always go hunting if you don't have anything."

"No!" Dirk spoke a little more forcefully than I think he meant to. He was, after all, talking to a dragon who could devour him with one bite. "I mean, it's better if you don't. If anyone sees you, they might think that you were here to attack them and attack you first. At least if I'm with you, I can explain to people that you don't mean any harm. Anyway, if you try to go anywhere by yourself, you might destroy more of Minecraftia and that really will get people fighting you just to protect their land." He rummaged around in his bag. "Look, I've got some mushrooms-"

"Yuck!"

"No? All right." He dug deeper. "What about some mutton? It's cold and a bit old, but it's still meat and it hasn't gone rotten yet."

He tossed it over and I caught it, chewing it up and swallowing. "Not bad."

"Good. Here's all the mutton I have. If I find any food nearby, I'll bring it back for you. If not, I'll try to be as quick as I can in getting you some new armor and we can go hunting together, OK?"

"OK," I agreed reluctantly as Dirk went to the other end of the ravine and started climbing back up to ground level.

I padded round in a circle, doing my best to make the ground comfortable while I settled down for a nap. I didn't like being in a big hole. It was as dark as The End, but without everything that made it home and there was nothing to see or do.

Some holiday this was turning out to be.

Day 10

Dirk was gone all night and still there was no sign of him when the morning came. I was woken up by the sound of my own belly rumbling, protesting at the lack of food. The few bits of mutton he'd left me last night hadn't gone very far and now I was starving.

It was no good. I was going to have to go off hunting, no matter what Dirk had said. Anyway, when I'd taken him flying, there hadn't been any sign of other humans. I'm sure it would be absolutely fine if I just popped out to get a cow or two or maybe a pig or chicken.

Since I had a landing pad already built, I decided to leave the rest of the armor in the hole I'd made. It felt so good to be flying without anything weighing me down.

I shot straight up into the sky, doing a little loop-de-loop in celebration. There must be another way of letting me move around Minecraftia that didn't involve stupid armor.

I gazed at the open plains beneath me. The sunflowers swayed gently in the breeze as I flew over them. I could see creatures moving around and as I swooped down, I realized that these were something I hadn't tried before. They whinnied and tried to get away from me, but I was too fast. Deftly, I grabbed one with my claws and carried it back to the ravine. Dropping it in the bottom, I settled down to enjoy my snack.

Bleuch! Horse meat does NOT taste nice!

"What are you doing?"

I looked up to see Dirk peering down from the top of the ravine.

"I thought I told you to stay where you were?"

"I was hungry!" I protested.

"Yes, well, you're lucky you didn't get shot at. Anything could have happened."

I frowned. "But there aren't any humans for miles around. I would have seen them. I was perfectly safe. Besides, I'm the Ender Dragon. I'm almost impossible to kill. If someone had been dumb enough to attack me, they would have quickly learned what a bad mistake they'd made."

"Even so, I think we should lay low for a while." Dirk climbed down the sides of the ravine. "We don't want to attract any more attention."

"If you say so. Did you bring me any food?"

Day 11

"Right. I'm going to go and put some armor together for you," Dirk told me. "I was able to scout about for possible resources and I know where I'm going now. It's a bit further than I thought, which is why I came back. I wanted you to know that I'm going to be gone for a couple of days while I get together everything I need, so I'm going to bring down some horses for you to snack on."

"Not horses!" I started heaving, pretending to be throwing up so that Dirk could see just how much I hated the idea of living off horses for a few days.

Dirk sighed heavily. "You could be a bit more grateful, you know. I've been doing my best to make sure you get a brilliant holiday. It's not my fault you decided to throw away some perfectly good armor."

"And it's not my fault that you're too heavy for me to carry with all that armor on," I countered. "Besides, if Minecraftia wasn't so flimsy it would be able to cope with me being here. You can't blame me for being so awesome that even the ground disappears out of fear."

"All right. I'll see if I can get some cows or pigs instead. But please, Ember, stay in the hole this time. It's for your own good."

"It's boring down here," I grumped. "I still don't see why I can't just fly you back to where we dropped the armor. That would be so much easier than my having to sit around, twiddling my thumbs while you try to sort something out."

"We've been over this. We can't risk you creating another big ravine when you land. Just stay here and I'll be as quick as I can. Promise."

Dirk climbed up the side of the ravine and soon after, a couple of pigs and cows came flying through the air, landing with a crash at the bottom of the hole.

"Back soon!" I heard him call as he raced off.

He'd better be. If he thinks that this is enough food to keep me full for long, he's sadly mistaken.

Day 12

This is so boring. I've tried counting how many layers there are up to the plains. I've been trying to imagine there are pictures in the clouds. I've even pretended that the pigs can talk so I can have a conversation, but none of that makes up for the fact that I'm stuck in the bottom of a hole with nothing to do and no one to talk to.

That's it. If Dirk isn't back by tomorrow, I'm going to fly off and explore by myself. I'm sure I can find somewhere to land that won't leave a gaping hole.

Day 13

"There it is! Are you ready lads? One, two, three?"

I was woken up by the cries of Minecraftians. Rubbing my eyes, I was too slow to wake up to realize what was going on until suddenly I felt something being thrown over me.

"It's worked! The net's worked! Now we can kill the Ender Dragon and get its eggs!"

Kill me? Take my eggs? No way was I going to let that happen.

I roared and stretched my wings. The net that was covering me snapped and tore and I was free to fly.

I shot straight into the sky, looking down at the panicking Minecraftians as they scrambled to find their weapons. A couple of them threw spears at me, spears I guessed that they would have used to hurt me if I'd stayed tangled in the net.

Roaring, I flew straight at them, snapping the spears as if they were twigs and zooming back up into the air. "I am Ember! Hear me roar!"

I swooped back down, sending Minecraftians flying with a flap of my wings. There was a scream as one of them fell down in the ravine. Served him right. How dare they attack me in my sleep? Didn't they know I was supposed to be on holiday?

I roared again, the final sound the Minecraftians were ever going to hear as I made short work of them.

"There," I said, flapping my wings to stay in the air so I wouldn't damage any more of the plains. "That will teach you to think you can attack the Ember Dragon when I'm on holiday."

There was no reply.

Day 14

"What on earth happened here?"

Dirk looked horrified as he climbed down into the ravine.

"A group of Minecraftians thought they could take me on. They were wrong." I shrugged, but I couldn't help but feel proud of myself. There had been many of them and it still hadn't been enough.

"I told you not to go flying," Dirk wailed. "This is what happens. They must have seen you in the air and come after you."

He looked at the remains of the net lying on the ground. "And what's this?"

"They threw a net over me," I explained. "I think they thought it was some kind of special net that could hold me, but nothing can hold the Ember Dragon. I am too powerful!"

Dirk fingered the net. "I see what they did here. It's been soaked in a potion of strength. Interesting idea. I read about it in *Secrets of successful Ender Dragon combat*. I guess they must have read the same book."

"Yet another book written by someone who doesn't know what they're talking about," I shrugged. "You people are so stupid to think that you can discover how to beat the Ender Dragon in a book."

"So how can you beat an Ender Dragon?" asked Dirk.

I glared at him.

"I just thought that it might make an interesting little detail for the book," he explained hurriedly.

"I told you. You can't learn how to beat me just by reading a book. I *will* say, though, that you can't beat me with a net and spear, so you can put that in your book if you like."

"I will," nodded Dirk. "Anyway, I've managed to make you some new armor, so if you want to put it on, we can get going."

This armor was even heavier than the last lot. "I'm going to be exhausted after a day of flying with this on," I complained.

"You'll get used to it," Dirk reassured me. "Now have you thought about where you'd like to go next?"

"I want to get a closer look at the mountains," I replied. "I want to know what that white stuff is."

"The white stuff? Oh, you mean snow. You'll like snow," Dirk told me. "We could have a snowball fight!"

"Are you sure you want to fight the Ender Dragon? I never lose, you know."

"We shall see," smirked Dirk.

Day 15

"You could have warned me about how cold snow is!" I complained, shivering so much that my armor bashed and crashed against itself, making a noise so loud I had to shout to be heard over it.

"I thought you knew!" yelled Dirk. "Everyone knows that snow is really cold. Heads up!"

Splat! A round ball of white, cold slush landed right on my nose. "Ow!" I protested. "What did you do that for?"

"This is a snowball fight," explained Dirk. "It's fun! Come on! Throw one back at me."

Glaring at him, I grabbed a handful of snow, packing it into a ball and throwing it back at Dirk.

"Missed me!" he laughed, throwing more snowballs back at me. Every one of them landed on me, making me even colder. For once, I was glad to be wearing the armor.

Without it, I would have been covered in snow. I might freeze to death!

I tried to get Dirk with a snowball, but I was a terrible shot. Dirk had a clear advantage, since I was so much bigger, so it was easier to hit me.

"No fair! You're too small for me to hit!"

"So are you saying that you've lost the fight?" laughed Dirk, throwing even more snowballs.

"The Ender Dragon never loses!"

A snowball in the face shut me up.

"All right! All right! You win! I give up! Just stop throwing those horrible snowballs at me."

I held my hands up in surrender and Dirk finally stopped bombarding me with snowballs.

"I hate snow," I grumbled. "Can we go somewhere warm instead?"

"Sure," Dirk replied. "It's getting late and we won't be able to see where we're going, so we'll need to camp here overnight, but in the morning we can head towards the desert if you like. It's very sunny there."

"Good. Let's get up early and go to the desert. I've had enough snow to last a lifetime."

The sooner we were out of the mountains and away from the freezing cold snow, the better.

Day 16

"That's it! Keep digging! Bury it deeper!"

I blinked my eyes open, but couldn't see anything. Was it night? Was I back in The End?

"More snow! Put more snow on!"

The voices filtered through and I realized what was happening. Minecraftians were burying me in snow!

I tried to roar, but all I got was a mouthful of snow. I tried to spread my wings, but with all the armor on me, I couldn't get up the strength to push the snow away. It was just too heavy.

Was this how I was going to die? Buried under a mountain of snow?

No. I am an Ender Dragon. We never give up and we're never defeated. I was going to find a way out of here.

I burped, just as I usually did when I first woke up. A little flame came out and when it touched the snow, the white stuff sizzled and evaporated.

That was it! I could burp my way out of the snow!

Luckily, I'm one of those gifted people who can burp whenever they want so I took a deep gulp and let out the loudest, longest belch I'd ever done.

BURP!

Soon, I was standing in a puddle of melted snow, surrounded by some very worried looking Minecraftians.

"I am Ember the Ender Dragon! Hear me roar!" I flapped my wings and without the snow holding me down, I soon rose up into the air, ready to pounce on the Minecraftians who'd tried to destroy me.

Three of them were so frightened that they threw themselves off the mountaintop rather than try and fight me.

"Stop trying to kill me!" I yelled at the Minecraftians, as I swooped over their heads. "I'm supposed to be on holiday!"

The Minecraftians looked at each other and shrugged before running away.

"And don't come back!" I called after them. Perhaps I should have killed them all, but this was the second time

I'd been ambushed. If I let some of them live, they might realize that they didn't stand a chance against me, and they'd tell anyone else who was thinking of coming after me not to waste their time.

As I calmed down from the excitement of the fight, I noticed that I hadn't seen Dirk for a while.

"Dirk? Dirk? Where are you?"

Nothing.

"Dirk?"

I was starting to panic, when I finally heard him calling to me. "Over here, Ember!"

I flew over to a mound of snow. Dirk was trying to claw his way out of it. I reached over with my wing and he grabbed hold so I could pull him out.

"Thanks, Ember," he said. "Those Minecraftians buried me under the snow so I couldn't come to help you. I'm glad you managed to fight them off. I was getting worried."

"Not even snow can defeat me!" I boasted.

"No, it doesn't look like it can."

Day 17

I couldn't wait to leave those mountains as far behind me as possible. I was sick of being cold, and being cold was making me sick. A-choo!

I have now learned that if I sneeze, I also send out a little flame, just like when I burp. Although sending out flames is really cool, having a cold really isn't.

The cold mountains gave way to lush jungle, which was a relief. It was a lot hotter here, but despite the warmth from the sun, I couldn't stop shivering. Was I ever going to get warm again?

I was feeling too weak to even fly and I dropped to the ground, walking next to Dirk.

"Are you all right, Ember?" he asked.

"Not really. My head is hurting, my throat is sore, and my nose is all sutffed up. I don't know why I ever thought it would be a good idea to go to the mountains. I feel like I'm going to die!"

"Don't be so silly," Dirk laughed. "It's just a cold. Tell you what, we'll make camp and I'll see if I can bring you a lot of food to help you get your strength up. I'll get a fire going and I'll even build a shelter around you so you can just curl up and get some sleep. How does that sound?"

"Thanks, Dirk."

"This looks like a good spot." Dirk led the way to a clearing and I sank to the floor as he quickly gathered up the wood for a fire. Soon, he had a nice little campfire going, but the heat from the flames barely reached me. I couldn't stop shivering and Dirk looked at me in concern as he started to put up a shelter around me.

"I'm really worried about you, Ember," he said. "You really don't look good."

"I really don't feel good," I replied. "I'm just going to curl up here and try to get some rest."

The moment my head touched the ground, I was asleep, my dreams haunted by nightmares of Minecraftians standing over me, cheering as they stole my eggs.

Day 18

"How are you feeling, Ember?" Dirk bent over me, putting a hand to my forehead. "You know, I have no idea why I'm feeling your forehead. I have no idea how hot or cold an Ender Dragon is supposed to feel!"

I tried to laugh, but my chuckle descended into a coughing fit that took over my body. "I'm still not great," I replied. "In fact, I think I'm feeling worse. I keep drifting in and out of sleep and thinking that I'm seeing Minecraftians coming to attack me. Look! There's one now."

I nodded at the bushes where I could see the figure of a Minecraftian. He ducked down behind the bushes when I pointed at him, so when Dirk turned around, there was nothing to see.

"Poor you. You're so sick you're imagining things. Well, I've found a lake near here, so I thought I'd go fishing. Fish might help you get better and it tastes amazing. Will you be all right if I leave you here?"

"I'll be fine. I'm the Ender Dragon, remember?" I tried to roar, but all that came out was a pathetic little squeak.

"OK, I'll try not to be too long. I've put plenty of wood on the fire to keep you warm and when I come back, we'll toast some fish together."

"Fine." I snuggled back down in the shelter Dirk had built for me and tried to get some more sleep, but I couldn't stop thinking about the Minecraftian in the bushes. Looking over to where I'd last seen him, I was sure that I saw other Minecraftians moving around in the undergrowth.

I shook my head and closed my eyes. I really was ill if I was seeing so many people all over the place. If Minecraftians were sneaking up on me, Dirk would have sounded the alert. There's no way he would have missed that many people.

"There it is! Kill the Ender Dragon! Get her eggs!"

"Are you kidding me?" Groaning, I dragged myself to my feet. "Can't I get some peace for five seconds? I'm ill! Leave me alone, why can't you?"

The only answer was an arrow shot at my wing.

"You leave me no choice."

Summoning every ounce of strength I had, I rushed out of the shelter. Some of my armor got caught on the wall and came off. I reached out to hit a Minecraftian and lost my balance. As my wing touched the ground beneath him, it disappeared, creating a hole that he fell into.

"Ow! Ow! My leg!" I heard him cry.

That gave me an idea. Instead of attacking the Minecraftians, I went for the ground beneath them and soon I was surrounded by Minecraftians rolling around on the floor, clutching where they'd injured themselves falling into the potholes I'd made.

"Look, I really don't want to kill you. I'm on holiday and I want a break from all that. But if you keep coming after me, you leave me no choice. This is your last warning. LEAVE ME ALONE!"

At last, my roar came back. I was starting to get better.

I watched as the Minecraftians helped each other up and limped off through the jungle.

"What happened here?" At last, Dirk came back with a string of fish. "Where did all these holes in the ground come from?"

"How could you have missed it?" I gasped. "I told you I'd seen a Minecraftian. I wasn't imagining it! A whole group of them attacked me. I was too weak to fight properly, so I made holes in the ground with my wing. My armor fell off while I was coming out of the shelter and there wasn't time to put it back on."

"Good thinking." Dirk helped strap the missing piece back on to my wing so I could sit by the campfire safely.

"I don't understand why you didn't see the Minecraftians coming, though," I went on. "Didn't you hear the sound of the fight? They were screaming so loudly it gave me a headache!"

"That must have been when I fell in the water," Dirk told me. "There was one fish that was really strong and it pulled me right in."

"But your clothes are dry," I frowned.

"I put them out in the sun," Dirk replied. "They dried out pretty quickly."

"I suppose it is rather warm here."

"Anyway, don't you want some of the fish I caught? I think you'll really like it."

Dirk started cooking the fish and he was right. I did really like it. All the same, I couldn't help thinking that there was something not quite right about his story. Something... fishy.

Day 19

I woke up feeling a lot better. Clearly a fish supper is the best way to help Ender Dragons get over colds. I still wasn't feeling up to travelling much though, so Dirk took me to the lake where he caught the fish.

"Want to try some fishing?" he offered.

It took a while to figure out how to hold the rod when the armor made it difficult for me to sit back, but in the end, I put it in my mouth and just yanked out the fish as soon as they nibbled.

Soon, we had a large pile of fish to eat. This was the best day of my holiday so far. Nobody attacked me, it wasn't freezing cold, and I just got to hang out with my new friend, Dirk.

Perfect!

Day 20

"Do you want to move on to the desert today?" asked Dirk. "It's even warmer there."

"That sounds like a great idea," I smiled. "I'm feeling a lot better now. I might even fly a little bit today."

Dirk packed up our camp and we set off towards the desert.

"You might have to be careful when we leave the jungle," warned Dirk. "There's a village not far from here and they won't know that you're on holiday, so if they see you, they might start attacking you or even send their iron golems after you."

"Well, they should know that I'm on holiday," I declared. "I keep telling everyone who attacks me that I'm on vacation in the hope that they'll leave me alone. You'd think they'd be grateful for not killing them, but no. They have to keep ambushing the Ender Dragon. It's making it very difficult to enjoy your beautiful world."

And Minecraftia was truly beautiful. I had no idea it was so lovely. It made me think of my home back in The End and wonder what I could do to make it a little brighter.

Perhaps I could take some seeds with me, try to grow some flowers. Sunflowers around my nest would look lovely and maybe if I hung up a large lamp, the plants would think it was the sun.

The more I thought about it, the more I liked the idea. I decided to start collecting seeds from every biome I visited as a little memento of my trip.

Day 21

"Here it is! The mighty desert!"

I gazed around me in awe. The jungle ended abruptly and the muddy ground gave way to sand that was almost hot enough to burn my feet as I walked over it. Strange prickly plants dotted about and when I touched one in curiosity, it drew blood.

"Ouch!"

"That's why we don't touch cacti, silly," laughed Dirk. "Now I've brought plenty of water with me, so we should be fine to cross the desert. There's a village a day or so walk from here. I'll let you decide whether you think it's a good idea to go there or if you'd prefer to avoid it."

I thought about it for a moment. "I know you said that they might attack me, but I really would like to see at least one village while I'm up here. I have no idea what your human towns are like. If it looks like they're going to attack, I could just fly away. Or even better, fly really high so they don't see me while I have a look at what it's like."

"I really wouldn't fly unless you absolutely have to," warned Dirk. "After all, you've only just recovered from your cold, so you're not at full strength and if you fly high enough to stay out of range of the arrows, you're not really going to be able to see all the details of the village, are you?"

"True, true."

Dirk thought for a moment. "There is one other option," he said at last. "But you might not like it."

"What?"

"Well, if you let me tie you up, put you in a cage and pretend that I've captured you, they won't think you're a threat."

"But then I won't be able to see the village either, will I?" I pointed out. "I'll be stuck in a cage."

"I can get some horses to pull the cage along," Dirk suggested. "That way, I can take you all over the village and make sure you see everything you want to before taking you out again, and you'll be completely safe because nobody will think you can get out. They won't know that you're a tourist and the cage is meant to protect you from them, not the other way round."

"It's definitely an interesting idea." I wanted to humor Dirk, but I couldn't see how this would work. Go in a cage? I didn't know that I really wanted to see a village badly enough to agree to being locked up.

Day 22

"Ta-daa!" Dirk looked so proud of his handiwork. I didn't have the heart to tell him I hated it. After he'd come up with the idea for the cage, he'd rushed into the jungle and started gathering resources to build it. He'd worked so hard for so long, I felt that I had to at least try going into the cage. He'd really gone out of his way to make this holiday a good one – I wouldn't even be here if it wasn't for him.

"It's… er… it's a cage! I mean… it's really good, Dirk."

His face fell. "You hate it."

"No, no. For a cage, it's really good. It's just that the whole idea of a cage is really difficult for me to deal with. Ender Dragons weren't meant to be in cages."

"I know that, but this is a special situation. You want to know what it's like inside a Minecraftian village, don't you?"

"I do…" But I wasn't sure I wanted to know badly enough that I'd climb into a cage.

"Look, if it makes you feel any better, I'll sprinkle this perfume all over the cage." Dirk pulled out a bottle from his bag. "Take a sniff and tell me what you think."

He pulled out the stopper and I took a deep breath. "It does smell rather nice," I admitted.

"Right. So I'll just pour this all over the cage and when you're inside, you'll feel as though you're in a comfy nest. You won't even notice the bars around you."

He climbed up to the top of the cage and sprinkled the potion all over it. "There you go! It's not every Ender Dragon who can say that they've had a cage custom built for them."

No Ender Dragon would want to say that they'd had a cage custom built for them, but I didn't tell Dirk that, not after all the trouble he'd gone to for me.

I climbed inside and curled up. As long as I didn't want to stretch my wings, it would be all right. I could certainly cope with it while I was touring the village.

I got out again. "All right. I'll stay in the cage while we visit the village. I just hope it doesn't take too long to see everything. My wings are going to get really cramped if I stay in there for too long."

Day 23

"When you said the cage would be portable, I didn't think you meant that *I* was going to be the one moving it around," I grumbled, as I shoved the cage through the sand. "This is really hard work!"

"Don't worry," soothed Dirk. "When we get closer to the village, I'll go ahead and fetch some help to carry you. I'm sure they can spare a few iron golems to parade you around. Imagine that! You'll be given your own personal tour of the village on the backs of golems. It'll be amazing!"

"Yeah, that's assuming that I've got enough energy to keep my eyes open by the time we get there," I complained. "You try pushing a heavy cage through sand in the boiling hot sun when you're wearing armor made out of rock! You couldn't do it for five seconds let alone for five hours."

"All right. If you really need a rest, we can set up camp for the night," Dirk said. "We're not far from the village anyway, so we can have some food and you can sleep in the cage tonight, try it on for size. I've still got some fish from the jungle and I know how much you love fish."

It was true. I did love fish and I was trying to figure out how I could get my hands on some once I was back in The End. If I was asked about my favorite part of Minecraftia, I would have to say the food. I'd never eaten so much delicious meat in all my life. I was really going to miss it all when I went back home.

Dirk got a campfire going and soon the pair of us were sitting around, happily munching on freshly cooked fish.

"You know I'm going to have to go back home soon," I told him. "I dread to think what all those Endermen have been doing without me while I've been gone. I'll probably go back and find the place in a complete mess."

"I'm sure it's all fine," Dirk reassured me. "You worry too much. You should relax and enjoy the break."

"Even so, I think I'll go home after we've visited the village. You should have more than enough material for your book, and after all the times I've been ambushed here, I'm looking forward to some peace and quiet again."

"All right. If that's what you want."

I yawned. "It is. Anyway, I'm going to go to bed now. I'll see you in the morning."

I climbed into the cage and curled up. It was definitely more comfortable here than lying on the itchy sand, but that wasn't saying much. Still, if this was going to let me explore a village, I could put up with it for one day. Just as long as it was only one day.

"I'll close the door behind you, just to keep you safe," Dirk said. "First thing in the morning, I'll run on ahead and get some help to carry you into the village. It's going to be so much fun!"

Day 24

I woke up and tried to stretch my wings.

CLANG!

They hit the side of the cage. I'd forgotten I'd let Dirk shut me in here overnight. "Hey, Dirk. Do you think you could let me out for a bit? I need to stretch out. My wings are feeling cramped."

No reply.

"Dirk? Can you open up the cage door?"

Nothing.

I guessed that he must have gone to the village to get help transporting the cage. He could have let me out for a fly first.

I shuffled about, trying to get comfortable, but it was impossible. Dirk hadn't made the cage big enough for me to move.

There was nothing else I could do. I was going to have to break out of the cage. Dirk would understand. I'm sure it wouldn't take him long to fix it once he came back.

"Sorry Dirk," I muttered, as I threw myself against the cage door, confident I could break it easily.

CLANG!

OUCH!

I had a very, very sore wing. The cage door didn't even budge.

It was all very strange.

I tried again and again to break the cage, but I didn't even make a dent in the bars. I know that Dirk had wanted to build something that looked like it could hold an Ender Dragon, but I didn't think that he was going to make something that really *could* hold an Ender Dragon. I didn't think that anything could contain me!

I didn't have any choice. I was going to have to wait for Dirk to come back and get me.

Day 25

"And here it is! Behold! The fabled Ender Dragon!"

I opened an eye at the sound of Dirk's voice. "Where have you been, Dirk? I've been stuck in this cage all day and all night and I haven't had anything to eat or drink. I'm wasting away!"

"Good."

Dirk put his face close to the bars of the cage. "Maybe now we'll be able to kill you," he hissed.

"Kill me? What are you talking about? Dirk, what's going on?"

"You know, I thought Ender Dragons were supposed to be intelligent." Dirk started walking round the cage, making it difficult for me to watch him all the way round. For the first time, I realized that he wasn't alone. I was sure that I recognized some of the Minecraftians who'd attacked me in the mountains and the jungle.

"I've been putting up with your company for almost a whole month and the more time I spend with you, the more I'm convinced that you're really, really dumb. Difficult to kill, yes, but really stupid. Thanks to you, I'm going to be able to write the most popular book ever on how to kill the Ender Dragon because I'm going to be the one Minecraftian author who's actually done it."

"I don't understand, Dirk. I thought we were friends!"

"Oh my poor, sweet Ember. You really thought that I would want to be friends with you? The only thing I want from you are your eggs and as soon as I've slaughtered you, they will be mine, all mine!"

"My eggs?" I started laughing and once I'd started I couldn't stop.

"What's so funny?" Dirk banged on the side of the cage. "Ember! What's so funny?"

"You can kill me as much as you want. You'll never get my eggs!"

Dirk tried to get me to explain what I meant, but I wasn't going to tell him anything. "All right, lads. Let's get this cage out of here. It's just a bluff. Once we've killed Ember and sold the eggs, we'll be rich!"

The cage lurched as all the Minecraftians came together to lift it up. Wherever we were going, it wasn't somewhere I wanted to be.

Day 26

It was the Minecraftians' turn to complain about how heavy the cage was, and I couldn't help but laugh as they moaned about how tough it was to push a cage with an armor clad Ender Dragon in it. Of course, Dirk didn't help them. He just sat back, barking out orders.

"Come on, men!" he shouted. "Think of all the emeralds and diamonds we're going to get once we've persuaded the Ender Dragon to tell us where the eggs are. We'll be swimming in them, rich beyond our wildest dreams!"

"You don't have to listen to Dirk, you know," I said to the Minecraftians. "It doesn't matter what he's promised you. He won't be able to get my eggs and even if he did, I guarantee he wouldn't share them with you. Just look at how he's betrayed me. Do you really think he won't do the same to you?"

"Don't listen to it, lads," countered Dirk, as some of them stopped pushing the cage to hear what I was saying. "It's just a dragon in a cage, trying to escape when it knows that we've won! I promise you that by the time I'm finished, it will be begging us to take the eggs just to make me stop torturing it."

Torture? I didn't like the sound of that. I needed to get out of this cage before we got to wherever it was we were going.

I started throwing myself around the cage, banging against the bars with all my might, but it was no good.

"Silly dragon," chuckled Dirk. "I've soaked the bars with a potion of strength. On top of that, I combined bedrock, obsidian, and diamond with a bit of Nether quartz ore to make this the strongest cage Minecraft has ever seen. It's impossible for you to escape. Go on. Try as much as you like. You'll never break free."

I roared and threw myself at the bars again, ripping off bits of armor with my teeth and throwing them, anything to get out.

"Why, thank you Ember," smiled Dirk as he collected up the bits of armor and tossed them away. "The more armor you remove, the lighter you are and the easier it is for my men to move the cage. It doesn't matter what you do – you're just making it simpler for me to get what I want. Of course, you could just save us all this trouble and tell me where your eggs are. I might even let you go if you did."

"Never! I'll die before I let you take my eggs."

"As you wish."

Day 27

When Dirk and I had gone to the desert, we'd taken our time to explore. After all, I was supposed to be on holiday, so as part of pretending to be my friend, Dirk had gone out of his way to show me all the fun stuff there was to do.

This time, there was no messing about. Dirk and his men travelled as quickly as they could, taking turns to push and carry the cage so that we didn't stop to rest until nightfall.

"Have you figured out where we're going yet?" grinned Dirk as we set up camp in the heart of the jungle.

I just growled at him. I was so mad I couldn't even speak.

"It's your favorite place! We might even build a snow dragon in your honor."

I looked to where he was pointing and my heart sank. We were heading straight back to the mountains.

I didn't know if I could cope with the cold again. Last time I'd felt so unwell, I thought I was going to die. Maybe this time, Dirk was relying on my getting sick again. He'd be able to kill me without lifting a finger – the mountains would do all the work for him.

"You could save yourself all this trouble if you just told me where your eggs are," Dirk said, putting his face close to the bars. "Once I've got my hands on a dragon egg or two, I might even let you go free. You can always lay another one. One little egg can't be that important, can it?"

He jumped back, laughing, as I tried to bite him through the bars.

"Temper, temper," he warned. "Oh well. Have it your way. We'll be at the mountains tomorrow and then you'll either tell me where you've hidden your eggs or we'll beat it out of you. We can do it the easy way or we can do it the hard way, but by the end of the day, I *will* have an Ender Dragon egg in my hands."

He walked off, leaving me alone with my thoughts. There had to be a way out of this cage. There just had to be. This was not how my story was going to end.

Day 28

"It's all right. We don't need to go too high," Dirk instructed his men. "Just high enough so that the dragon starts feeling the cold. We can then start packing the cage with snow. She'll soon start talking."

Snow? "You can't do this!" I cried. "I'm the Ender Dragon! At least let me out so we can fight fairly!"

"Fight fairly?" Dirk laughed. "Even with twenty men, it's not a fair fight and you know it. No, I like you just where you are. This is the only way we're going to beat you."

I tried to bash my way out of the cage again, but I'd barely eaten for the past couple of days and with the temperature steadily dropping, there was no way I was going to escape.

Dirk had won. The fight was over before it had even begun.

"OK, then, lads. Put the cage down."

The cage dropped with a thud, jolting every bone in my body.

"This is your last chance," Dirk warned. "Tell us where the eggs are or we're going to bury you in snow."

I hung my head. "Do your worst. I won't give you my eggs."

The first snowball hit me and a cheer went up from the men. "Bet you I get it right on the wing!" yelled one, before throwing his snowball. "Bullseye!"

That was the cue for everyone to start throwing snow at me as fast as they could. A flurry of snowballs came at me from all sides and I could feel myself getting colder and colder as the snow covered more and more of my body. I tried shaking it off at first, but there was just too much snow being thrown at me.

It covered my legs, my tail, my wings until all that was left was the tip of my snout poking out above the snow.

"Tell me where the egg is or you will die in a cage on a mountain," Dirk said.

"Goodbye, Dirk."

"If that's the way you want it." Dirk picked up a handful of snow and the last thing I saw was him packing it down on my face.

Everything went black.

Day 29

"Ember! Ember! Wake up, Ember! Are you all right?"

"Where am I?" Slowly, I blinked my eyes, trying to figure out what had happened. The last thing I remembered was being buried under a ton of snow.

"It's me, Jo. You're back in the End."

"I'm back in The End?" I sat up and looked around. It was true! I was back home! I wasn't dead! "What happened? How did I get here?"

"You were gone for so long that we were starting to worry, so we decided to come looking for you. Some of the other Endermen and I teleported up to Minecraftia and started hunting around. Once we found that big hole in the plains you'd made, we were able to follow your tracks, and when we saw a group of Minecraftians dancing around a cage filled with snow, we knew that something was up. We chased the Minecraftians away and brought you back home. And it looks like we made it just in time too – you were very cold when we brought you back. You were hardly breathing."

"A-choo!" How annoying. I'd caught another cold. Still, it was a small price to pay for being back home, safe and sound. "What about the Minecraftians? What happened to them?"

"They ran away," Jo replied. "Good thing too. If they'd stuck around, we would have shown them exactly what happens to people who think they can hurt the Ender Dragon."

"Thanks, Jo. You're a true friend. Now I better go and check on my eggs. Dirk went to all that effort to try and steal them. I want to make sure that it wasn't just a distraction while someone came down here and took them."

I flapped my wings and flew high into the sky, off to my secret floating island. Nobody knows that it's there and you can only get to it by flying, but Dirk had shown himself to be such a sneaky person, I didn't trust him not to have figured out a way to get to them.

I landed and breathed a huge sigh of relief. My eggs were all there, safe and sound. I picked up one, giving it a big hug. "There, my baby. You're safe. I'm not going to let anything happen to you."

Putting it back with the others, I went for a fly around The End. Everything was just as I'd left it. Why had I been so stupid as to go on holiday when everything I need is right here?

Day 30

"Whomp!"

It was the sound of a Minecraftian arriving in the end. I shook my head and went to see who it was. After everything I'd been through, I was in no mood to deal with any more Minecraftians.

I couldn't believe it. "Dirk! You've got some nerve coming here." I made to swoop at him.

"Wait! Don't hurt me!" He held his hands out and I could see that he was carrying something. "I brought this for you."

He held it out to me and I could see it was a book. Taking it, I read the title. *Adventures with Ember. The kindest, sweetest Ender Dragon who ever lived.*

"I've come to say I'm sorry," Dirk told me. "I don't know what came over me. I really did just want to have fun with you, but when I met those other Minecraftians, they persuaded me to try and steal your egg. I didn't want to, but they said they'd hurt me if I didn't."

I raised an eyebrow. "Did you think that I hatched yesterday?"

"No, honestly. It's true. It's all in the book. You can read about it. And don't worry. I didn't tell anyone about your problem with snow."

"It wouldn't matter if you did. I'm never going up to Minecraftia again and anyway, snow melts in The End. The big wet patch in your pocket is proof of that."

Dirk blushed. "You can't blame me for trying. Look, could I at least see a dragon egg, just so that I know that they exist?"

I roared at him so loudly that his hair stood on end and his clothes billowed in the wind.

"I'll take that as a no, then." Dirk straightened out his clothes. "Well, I'll leave you to it, then. I'm going back up to Minecraftia. I just wanted to say that I hoped that there are no hard feelings and maybe we could hang around together one day. I didn't get to show you the Extreme Hills or take you down the mines. And then there's the whole of the Nether to explore…"

"Goodbye, Dirk," I said firmly. "And this time, I mean it. If you ever come back to the End again, I'll kill you on sight – if the Endermen don't get to you first."

Dirk went pale. "All right, Ember. No need to be like that. I'm leaving and you won't see me again."

He went back to his portal and disappeared, but I had a funny feeling that he'd be back one day. Still, if he was stupid enough to return, I'd be waiting for him with an army of Endermen.

I settled down into my nest and started reading the book he'd left me. He was right. It was good having something different to read for a change. I really did have some exciting adventures!

97124024R00046

Made in the USA
Middletown, DE
04 November 2018